THE BIG BOOK OF
AUDITION SONGS
MORE HITS

WISE PUBLICATIONS
PART OF THE MUSIC SALES GROUP
LONDON / NEW YORK / PARIS / SYDNEY / COPENHAGEN / BERLIN / MADRID / HONG KONG / TOKYO

Published by

Wise Publications
14-15 Berners Street, London W1T 3LJ, UK

Exclusive Distributors:

Music Sales Limited
Distribution Centre, Newmarket Road,
Bury St Edmunds, Suffolk IP33 3YB, UK

Music Sales Pty Limited
20 Resolution Drive,
Caringbah, NSW 2229, Australia

Order No. AM999757
ISBN 978-1-84938-443-8
This book © Copyright 2010 Wise Publications,
a division of Music Sales Limited.

Edited by Jenni Wheeler.
Compiled by Nick Crispin.
CD recorded, Mixed & Mastered by Jonas Persson.
Cover designed by Liz Barrand.

Printed in the EU

www.musicsales.com

YOUR GUARANTEE OF QUALITY

As publishers, we strive to produce every book
to the highest commercial standards.
The music has been freshly engraved and the book has
been carefully designed to minimise awkward page turns
and to make playing from it a real pleasure.
Particular care has been given to specifying acid-free,
neutral-sized paper made from pulps which have not been
elemental chlorine bleached. This pulp is from farmed
sustainable forests and was produced with special regard
for the environment.
Throughout, the printing and binding have been planned
to ensure a sturdy, attractive publication which should
give years of enjoyment.
If your copy fails to meet our high standards,
please inform us and we will gladly replace it.

CD TRACK LISTING

CD 1

1. **CABARET**
   (EBB/KANDER) CARLIN MUSIC CORPORATION

2. **CALL ME**
   (HARRY/MORODER) CHRYSALIS MUSIC LIMITED/SONY/ATV HARMONY (UK) LIMITED

3. **CALL OFF THE SEARCH**
   (BATT) SONY/ATV MUSIC PUBLISHING (UK) LIMITED

4. **DON'T CHA**
   (CALLAWAY/RAY) NOTTING HILL MUSIC (UK) LIMITED

5. **GET THE PARTY STARTED**
   (PERRY) SONY/ATV HARMONY (UK) LIMITED

6. **HALLELUJAH**
   (COHEN) SONY/ATV MUSIC PUBLISHING (UK) LIMITED

7. **I DREAMED A DREAM**
   (SCHÖNBERG/BOUBLIL/NATEL/KRETZMER) ALAIN BOUBLIL MUSIC LIMITED

8. **I JUST WANT TO MAKE LOVE TO YOU**
   (DIXON) BUG MUSIC LIMITED/JEWEL MUSIC PUBLISHING COMPANY LIMITED

9. **I SHOULD BE SO LUCKY**
   (STOCK/AITKEN/WATERMAN) ALL BOYS MUSIC LIMITED/SONY/ATV MUSIC PUBLISHING (UK) LIMITED/
   UNIVERSAL MUSIC PUBLISHING LIMITED

10. **KISS KISS**
    (AKSU/JAIMES/WELTON-JAIMES) UNIVERSAL MUSIC PUBLISHING LIMITED/SONIC BOOM MUSIC

11. **LOVE SONG**
    (SARA BAREILLES) SONY/ATV MUSIC PUBLISHING (UK) LIMITED

12. **LISTEN**
    (KRIEGER/PREVEN/CUTLER/KNOWLES) EMI MUSIC PUBLISHING LIMITED/
    SONY/ATV HARMONY (UK) LIMITED/IMAGEM MUSIC/COPYRIGHT CONTROL

13. **9 TO 5**
    (PARTON) CARLIN MUSIC CORPORATION

CD 2

1. **THE NEARNESS OF YOU**
   (WASHINGTON/CARMICHAEL) SONY/ATV HARMONY (UK) LIMITED

2. **ONE DAY I'LL FLY AWAY**
   (JENNINGS/SAMPLE) UNIVERSAL MUSIC PUBLISHING LIMITED/CHRYSALIS MUSIC LIMITED

3. **PUT YOUR RECORDS ON**
   (BAILEY RAE/BECK/CHRISANTHOU) GOOD GROOVE SONGS LIMITED/GLOBAL TALENT PUBLISHING

4. **RISE**
   (DYLAN/GABRIELLE/UNGER-HAMILTON/DAGOIS)
   SONY/ATV MUSIC PUBLISHING (UK) LIMITED/PERFECT SONGS LIMITED/CHRYSALIS MUSIC LIMITED

5. **RESPECT**
   (REDDING) UNIVERSAL MUSIC PUBLISHING LIMITED/WARNER/CHAPPELL MUSIC LIMITED

6. **ROAD RAGE**
   (MATTHEWS/ROBERTS/RICHARDS/JONES/POWELL) SONY/ATV MUSIC PUBLISHING (UK) LIMITED

7. **TELL ME ON A SUNDAY**
   (WEBBER/BLACK) THE REALLY USEFUL GROUP LIMITED/UNIVERSAL/DICK JAMES MUSIC LIMITED

8. **SUPERSTAR**
   (BELMAATI/HANSEN/SIGVARDT) UNIVERSAL MUSIC PUBLISHING LIMITED/
   WARNER/CHAPPELL MUSIC LIMITED

9. **TAKE MY BREATH AWAY**
   (WHITLOCK/MORODER) WARNER/CHAPPELL MUSIC NORTH AMERICA/SONY/ATV HARMONY (UK) LIMITED

10. **WHAT'S UP?**
    (PERRY) SONY/ATV HARMONY (UK) LIMITED

11. **YOU HAD ME**
    (STONE/WRIGHT/WHITE/STOKER)
    UNIVERSAL MUSIC PUBLISHING MGB LIMITED/UNIVERSAL MUSIC PUBLISHING LIMITED

12. **UMBRELLA**
    (NASH/STEWART/HARRELL/CARTER)
    PEERMUSIC (UK) LIMITED/WARNER/CHAPPELL NORTH AMERICA LIMITED/
    SONY/ATV MUSIC PUBLISHING (UK) LIMITED/EMI MUSIC PUBLISHING LIMITED

To remove your CD from the plastic sleeve,
lift the small lip to break the perforations.
Replace the disc after use for convenient storage

CABARET

WORDS BY FRED EBB
MUSIC BY JOHN KANDER

1. What good is sit-ting a-lone in your room?
2. Put down the knit-ting, the book and the broom; it's

when I saw her laid out like a queen, she was the hap-pi-est corpse I'd ev-er seen. I think of Els-ie to this ver-y day. I re--mem-ber how she'd turn to me and say:

CALL ME

WORDS BY DEBORAH HARRY
MUSIC BY GIORGIO MORODER

16

18

CALL OFF THE SEARCH

WORDS & MUSIC BY MIKE BATT

world that I see to - day._____ And I've____ got a feel-ing

it won't fade a - way._____ 3. And I won't

end my days____ wish-ing____ that____ love would____ come a - long, 'cause

you____ are in my life where you be - long._____ Now_____ that I've found you I'll

call off the search.

Now that I've found you I'll

call off the search.

Now that I've found you I'll

call off the search.

DON'T CHA

WORDS & MUSIC BY THOMAS CALLAWAY
& ANTHONY RAY

GET THE PARTY STARTED

WORDS & MUSIC BY LINDA PERRY

start- ed.

D.S. al Coda

3. Mak - ing my con-

⊕ *Coda*

I'm_____ com-ing up so you bet - ter get this par - ty start - ed._

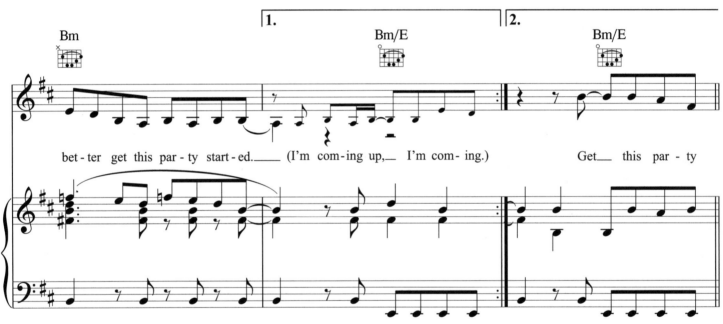

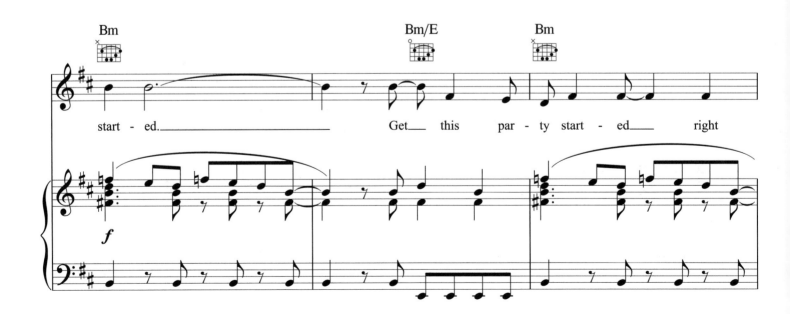

Verse 2:

Pumping up the volume, breaking down to the beat,
Cruising through the west side, we'll be checking the scene.
Boulevard is freaking as I'm coming up fast,
I'll be burning rubber you'll be kissing my Benz.
Pull up to the bumper, get out of the car,
License plates say stunning number one superstar.

I'm coming up *etc.*

Verse 3:

Making my connection as I enter the room,
Everybody's chilling as I set up the groove.
Pumping up the volume with this brand new beat,
Everybody's dancing and they're dancing for me.
I'm your operator, you can call any time,
I'll be your connection to the party line.

I'm coming up *etc.*

HALLELUJAH

WORDS & MUSIC BY LEONARD COHEN

2.

-lu - - - - - jah.

rall. **rit.**

a tempo

3. May - be there's a god a - bove,_ but all I've ev - er learned from love was

how to shoot some-bod - y_____ who out - drew ya. It's

38

I DREAMED A DREAM

MUSIC BY CLAUDE-MICHEL SCHÖNBERG
ORIGINAL LYRICS BY ALAIN BOUBLIL & JEAN-MARC NATEL
ENGLISH LYRICS BY HERBERT KRETZMER

so diff-'rent from this hell I'm liv - ing;____ so diff-'rent now from what it

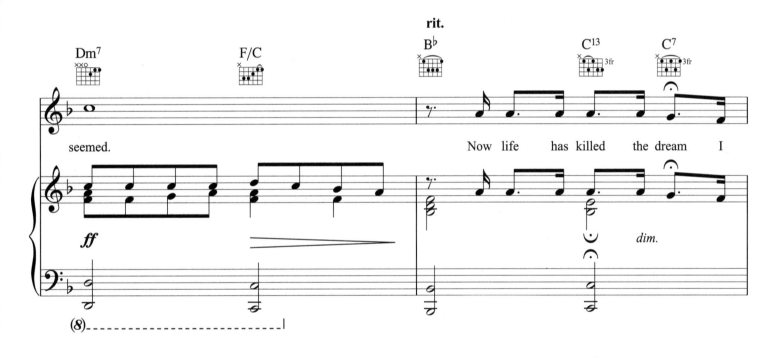

seemed. Now life has killed the dream I

dreamed.

I JUST WANT TO MAKE LOVE TO YOU

WORDS & MUSIC BY WILLIE DIXON

44

sad and blue_____ I just wan-na make_ love_ to you.

Love_ to you, oooh,_____ love_ to you

oooh._____

Verse 2:
All I want to do is wash your clothes,
I don't want to keep you indoors.
There is nothing for you to do,
But keep me making love to you.

I SHOULD BE SO LUCKY

WORDS & MUSIC BY MIKE STOCK,
MATT AITKEN & PETE WATERMAN

1. In my_

KISS KISS

WORDS & MUSIC BY SEZEN AKSU, JULIETTE JAIMES & STEVE WELTON-JAIMES

Mwah! 1. When you look at me, tell me what you see. This is what you get, it's the way I am.
(Verse 2 see block lyric)

When I look at you I wan-na be, I wan-na be some-where close to heav-en with Ne-an-der-thal man.

Don't go, I know you wan-na touch me, here, there and ev-'ry-where. Sparks fly when we are to-geth-er,

you can't de-ny the facts of life._____ You don't have to act like a star,_____ try-ing

moves in the back of your car._____ But you know that we can go far,_____ 'cause to-

Verse 2:
You could be mine baby, what's your star sign
Won't you take a step into the lions den?
I can hear my conscience calling me, calling me
Say I'm gonna be a bad girl again.
Why don't you come on over, we can't leave this all undone.
Got a devil on my shoulder, there's no place for you to run.

You don't have to act *etc.*

LOVE SONG

WORDS & MUSIC BY SARA BAREILLES

1. Head un-der-wa-ter and you tell___ me to breathe eas-
2. I learned the hard___ way that they all___ say things___

-y for a while.___ The breath-ing gets hard___ -er; e-ven I___
___ you wan-na hear. And my___ heav-y heart sinks deep___

61

LISTEN

WORDS & MUSIC BY HENRY KRIEGER, ANNE PREVEN,
SCOTT CUTLER & BEYONCÉ KNOWLES

9 TO 5

WORDS & MUSIC BY DOLLY PARTON

Jump in   the shower and the blood starts pump - ing,
In   the   same boat with a   lot   of   your friends,

out   on   the streets the traf - fic starts   jump - ing   with   folks
wait - ing   for   the   day   your   ship -'ll   come   in   and   the

__ like   me__ on the job   from   nine___ to five.___   Work - ing
__ tide's   gon - na turn and   it's   all gon - na row you a - way.

nine to___   five.___   What   a   way to make__ a liv - ing. Bare - ly

⊕ *Coda*

(1,3.) nine to___ five.___ What a way to make__ a liv - ing. Bare - ly
(2,4.) Nine to___ five,___ yeah, they got you where they want__ you, there's a

get - ting by,_____ it's all tak - ing and__ no giv - ing. They just
bet - ter life,_____ and you think a - bout__ it don't_ you? It's a

use___ your mind and you nev - er get__ the cred - it. It's e -
rich___ man's game, no mat - ter what they call___ it. And you

-nough to drive___ you cra - zy if___ you let___ it.___
spend your life put - ting mon - ey in___ his wal - let.

4° Fade

THE NEARNESS OF YOU

WORDS BY NED WASHINGTON
MUSIC BY HOAGY CARMICHAEL

ONE DAY I'LL FLY AWAY

WORDS BY WILL JENNINGS
MUSIC BY JOE SAMPLE

One day I'll fly a-way leave all this to yes-ter-day.

What more could your love do for me, when will love be through with me?

Why live life from dream to dream, and dread the day when

PUT YOUR RECORDS ON

WORDS & MUSIC BY CORINNE BAILEY RAE, JOHN BECK & STEVEN CHRISANTHOU

84

RISE

WORDS & MUSIC BY BOB DYLAN, GABRIELLE,
FERDY UNGER-HAMILTON & OLLIE DAGOIS

hopes, look at my dreams, I'm build-ing bridg-es from the scenes. Now I'm

read-y_____ to rise a-gain._____ (Mm.)_____

3. Much time____ has passed be-tween us,____ mm, do you still think of me____ at all?____

My world_____ of bro-ken prom-is-es_____

91

Verse 2:
Caught up in my thinking, yeah
Like a prisoner in my mind.
You pose so many questions
That the truth is hard to find.
I'd better think twice, I know
That I'll get over you.

Look at my life *etc.*

RESPECT

WORDS & MUSIC BY OTIS REDDING

Solid 4 Beat

1. What you want ba - by I got.
2. I ain't gon - na do you wrong while you gone.

What you need, you know I got it.
I ain't gon - na do you wrong, 'cause I don't wan - na.

in re - turn, hon - ey,   is to give me
so is my mon - ey,   all I want you to do for me

my prop - er re - spect   when you get home.   Yeah,
is give me some here   when you get home.   Yeah,

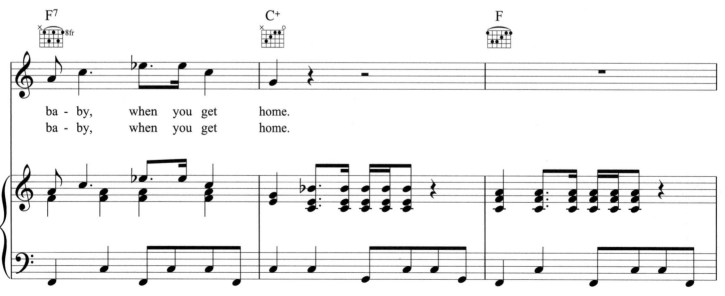

ba - by, when you get home.
ba - by, when you get home.

ROAD RAGE

WORDS & MUSIC BY CERYS MATTHEWS, MARK ROBERTS,
ALED RICHARDS, PAUL JONES & OWEN POWELL

come here,_ you_ can leave it late_ with me._

You could be tak-ing it eas - y on_ your-self; you should be mak-ing it eas-

- y on_ your-self._ 'Cause you and I_ know it's all o-ver the front_

_ page, you give me road_ rage, rac-ing through the best days. It's up to you_

104

TELL ME ON A SUNDAY

MUSIC BY ANDREW LLOYD WEBBER
LYRICS BY DON BLACK

F   Am⁷   Dm⁷   Em⁷   B♭ E♭/B♭ B♭

that's no way to end this. I know how I_____ want you to say good-bye; don't run

Am⁷/G   G⁷   Am⁷/G   G⁷   rit.

off in the pour-ing rain; don't call me as they call your plane; take the

Am⁷/G   F   **Tempo I** C/G   G⁷

hurt out of all the pain! Take me to a park that's

F B♭/F F   C/G   G⁷   C

cov-ered with trees,__ tell me on a Sun-day please.

SUPERSTAR

WORDS & MUSIC BY JOSEPH BELMAATI,
MICH HANSEN & MIKKEL SIGVARDT

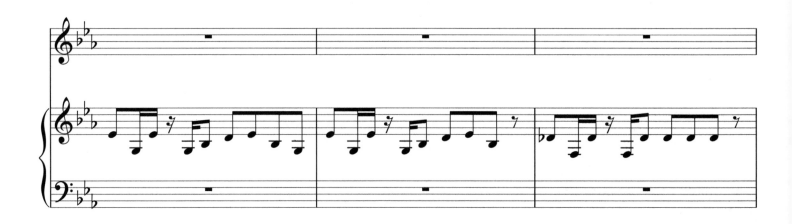

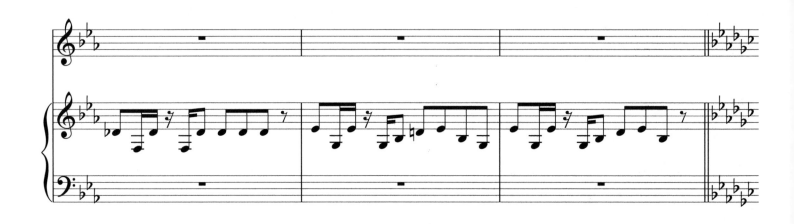

1. Peo - ple al - ways talk a - bout (Ey oh, ey oh, ey oh.)
2. Ba - by, take a look a - round, (Ey oh, ey oh, ey oh.)

all the things they're all a - bout. (Ey oh, ey oh, ey oh.)
ev - 'ry - bod - y's get - ting down. (Ey oh, ey oh, ey oh.)

Write it on a piece of pa - per.
Deal with all the prob - lems lat - er.

Got a feel - ing I'll see you lat - er.
Bad boys on their best be - hav - iour.

There's some-thing

I like the way you're mov - in'. (Ey oh, ey oh, ey oh.)

I just get in - to the groove and then... (You just make me wan - na play.)

If you just put pen to pa - per. (Ey oh, ey oh, ey oh.)

Got that feel - in' I'll see you la - ter. (Ey oh, ey oh, ey oh.) Make your_

move._____ Can't we get a lit-tle clos-er? You_____

rock it just like you're sup-posed to. Hey,_____

boy, I ain't got noth-ing more to say._____ 'Cause

you just make me wan-na play. I don't know what it is

TAKE MY BREATH AWAY

WORDS BY TOM WHITLOCK
MUSIC BY GIORGIO MORODER

1. Watch-ing ev-'ry mo-tion in____ my fool-ish lov-er's game;____
2. Watch-ing, I keep wait-ing, still____ an-tic-i-pat-ing love,____
3. Watch-ing ev-'ry mo-tion in____ this fool-ish lov-er's game;____

on this end-less o-cean, fi - n'lly lov-ers know no shame.____
nev-er hes-i-tat-ing to____ be - come the fat-ed ones.____
haunt-ed by the no-tion, some - where there's a love in flames.____

Turn-ing and re-turn-ing to____ some se-cret place in-side;____
Turn-ing and re-turn-ing to____ some se-cret place to hide;____
Turn-ing and re-turn-ing to____ some se-cret place in-side;____

watch-ing in slow mo-tion as____ you turn a-round and say,____
watch-ing in slow mo-tion as____ you turn to me and say,____ my love,} "Take my breath a-
watch-ing in slow mo-tion as____ you turn to me and say,

1.

To Coda

- way."   "Take my breath a-

121

WHAT'S UP

WORDS & MUSIC BY LINDA PERRY

126

YOU HAD ME

WORDS & MUSIC BY JOSS STONE, BETTY WRIGHT, EG WHITE & WENDY STOKER

I don't want you here, mess-ing with my mind.

I've real-ised in time that my eyes are not blind.

I've seen it be-fore; I'm tak-ing back my life.

You swore_ you had con-trol of it;___ when I___ stepped back,_ you slipped on your_ sup - ply.__

You had me,___ you lost me,___ you're wast - ed,___ you cost_ me.__

UMBRELLA

WORDS & MUSIC BY TERIUS NASH, CHRISTOPHER STEWART,
THADDIS HARRELL & SHAWN CARTER

Spoken: Uh-huh uh-huh, yeah, Rihanna. Uh-huh uh-huh, good

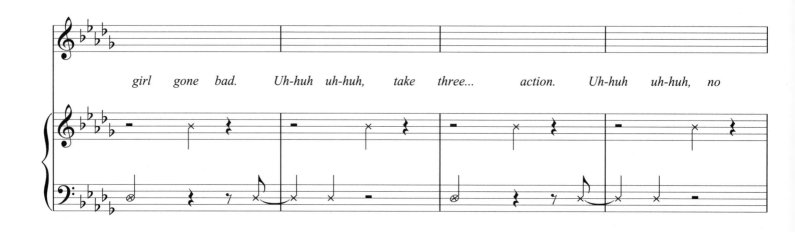

girl gone bad. Uh-huh uh-huh, take three... action. Uh-huh uh-huh, no

Eh eh eh,

clouds in my storms, let it rain, I hydroplane into fame, comin' down with the Dow Jones. When the